Visual Geography Series®

PAKISTAN

...in Pictures

Prepared by
Geography Department

Lerner Publications Company
Minneapolis

VISUAL GEOGRAPHY SERIES®

Publisher
Harry Jonas Lerner
Associate Publisher
Nancy M. Campbell
Senior Editor
Mary M. Rodgers
Editor
Gretchen Bratvold
Assistant Editors
Dan Filbin
Kathleen S. Heidel
Photo Researcher
Karen A. Sirvaitis
Editorial/Photo Assistant
Marybeth Campbell
Consultants/Contributors
Nathan Rabe
Sandra K. Davis
Designer
Jim Simondet
Cartographer
Carol F. Barrett
Indexer
Sylvia Timian
Production Manager
Gary J. Hansen

Independent Picture Service

Elaborate mosaics decorate an archway of Lahore Fort, which was built during the sixteenth century.

This book is an all-new edition of the Visual Geography Series. Previous editions were published by Sterling Publishing Company, New York City. The text, set in 10/12 Century Textbook, is fully revised and updated, and new photographs, maps, charts, and captions have been added.

LIBRARY OF CONGRESS CATALOGING-IN-PUBLICATION DATA

Pakistan in pictures.

(Visual geography series)
Rev. ed. of: Pakistan in pictures / prepared by Jon A. Teta.
Includes index.
Summary: Photographs and text introduce the geography, history, government, people, and economy of Pakistan.
1. Pakistan. [1. Pakistan] I. Teta, Jon A. Pakistan in pictures. II. Lerner Publications Company. Geography Dept. III. Series: Visual geography series (Minneapolis, Minn.)
DS376.9.P377   1989   954.9   88-13589
ISBN 0-8225-1850-3 (lib. bdg.)

International Standard Book Number: 0-8225-1850-3
Library of Congress Card Catalog Number: 88-13589

Independent Picture Service

A young Pakistani wears the style of woolen hat that Mohammed Ali Jinnah, the nation's founder, popularized.

Acknowledgments

Title page photo courtesy of Nathan Rabe.

Elevation contours adapted from *The Times Atlas of the World*, seventh comprehensive edition (New York: Times Books, 1985).

3 4 5 6 7 8 9 10 – JR – 03 02 01 00 99 98 97 96

Much of Pakistan's water supply is pumped to the surface from underground sources. Here, a camel activates a device – called a Persian wheel – that raises the water to ground level.

Contents

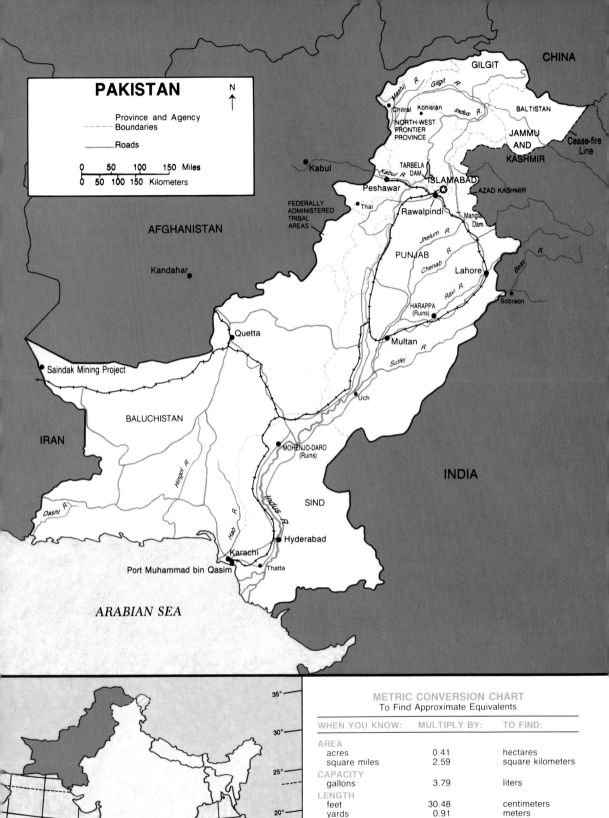

PAKISTAN

N ↑

Province and Agency Boundaries
Roads

0   50   100   150 Miles
0   50   100   150 Kilometers

CHINA

GILGIT

BALTISTAN

JAMMU AND KASHMIR

Cease-fire Line

Mastuj R.
Gilgit
Chitral Konistan Indus R.

NORTH-WEST FRONTIER PROVINCE

AZAD KASHMIR

Kabul

TARBELA DAM
Kabul R.
ISLAMABAD
Peshawar
Rawalpindi
Mangla Dam
Thal

FEDERALLY ADMINISTERED TRIBAL AREAS

Jhelum R.
PUNJAB
Chenab
Beas R.
Lahore
Ravi R.
Sobraon

AFGHANISTAN

Kandahar

HARAPPA (Ruins)

Quetta

Multan
Sutlej

Saindak Mining Project

Uch

BALUCHISTAN

IRAN

Hingol R.

MOHENJO-DARO (Ruins)

INDIA

Dasht R.

Hab R.
Indus R.

SIND

Hyderabad
Karachi
Port Muhammad bin Qasim
Thatta

ARABIAN SEA

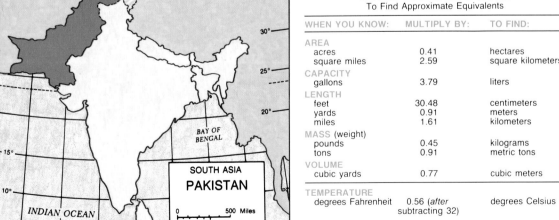

35°
30°
25°
20°
15°
10°
5°

BAY OF BENGAL

SOUTH ASIA
PAKISTAN

0   500 Miles
0   500 Kilometers

INDIAN OCEAN

65° 70° 75° 80° 85° 90° 95°

METRIC CONVERSION CHART
To Find Approximate Equivalents

WHEN YOU KNOW:	MULTIPLY BY:	TO FIND:
AREA		
acres	0.41	hectares
square miles	2.59	square kilometers
CAPACITY		
gallons	3.79	liters
LENGTH		
feet	30.48	centimeters
yards	0.91	meters
miles	1.61	kilometers
MASS (weight)		
pounds	0.45	kilograms
tons	0.91	metric tons
VOLUME		
cubic yards	0.77	cubic meters
TEMPERATURE		
degrees Fahrenheit	0.56 (*after* subtracting 32)	degrees Celsius

In northwestern Pakistan, travelers cross a suspension bridge – one of the longest in Asia – that spans the Gilgit River.

Introduction

Pakistan shares a long history with India, its eastern neighbor in south central Asia. The nation's eventful past includes ancient civilizations, such as the Indus culture that thrived in eastern Pakistan and western India between 2500 and 1800 B.C. Merchants from the Arabian Peninsula introduced the Islamic religion to the region in the seventh century A.D. Islam has since been a unifying force among Pakistan's many ethnic groups.

Pakistan was also the northwestern wing of the Mughal and the British empires. Both realms developed styles of administration, architecture, and education that have survived to modern times.

Beginning in the early twentieth century, Muslims (followers of Islam) in India

5

sought to establish a nation—called Pakistan—for themselves. These Muslims believed that India's Hindu religious majority had too much influence over Muslim culture and economic life. In August 1947 Pakistan became a reality when it achieved independence. The new nation was made up of two Muslim-dominated territories—West Pakistan and East Pakistan—which were separated by over 1,000 miles of Indian land.

Soon after gaining independence, Pakistan experienced several conflicts. It clashed with India over who would own Jammu and Kashmir, a region located along West Pakistan's border with India. In 1971 West Pakistan fought a civil war with East Pakistan that resulted in the latter becoming the independent nation of

In Chitral, northern Pakistan, faithful Muslims (followers of Islam) pause at noon to say their prayers.

Bangladesh. Military rulers have dominated over half of Pakistan's history as a self-governing country.

Although most of Pakistan's population follows the Islamic religion, Pakistanis retain strong ties with their various ethnic heritages. The most dominant group is the Punjabis, who inhabit much of the fertile agricultural land of the Indus River Valley. The southwestern area where the Baluchi live is rich in natural resources, particularly oil, natural gas, and copper. The Sindhi come from the farmlands of Sind province, and Pathans dwell in the rugged northwest.

Pakistan's leadership has yet to make these diverse ethnic communities into a unified nation in which Islam and democracy can coexist. Finding a national identity that satisfies all of the country's ethnic groups will be among Pakistan's challenges in the coming decades.

Islam—the main faith practiced in Pakistan—encourages women to wear full-length coverings, sometimes called burkas, as a form of modest dress.

K2 – the highest point in Pakistan – lies within the nation's portion of Jammu and Kashmir, a territory whose boundaries are disputed with India. The peak, which rises to 28,250 feet in the Karakoram Range, is the second tallest mountain in the world after Mount Everest. K2 has also been called Godwin Austen – after the British explorer who first surveyed it.

1) The Land

With over 300,000 square miles of territory, Pakistan is slightly larger than the state of Texas. It covers the northwestern portion of the southern Asian region known as the Indian subcontinent.

The Arabian Sea forms Pakistan's southern boundary, Iran lies to the southwest, and Afghanistan is located to the west and northwest. China lies to the northeast, and India stretches along Pakistan's eastern frontier. India and Pakistan disagree about their mutual boundary in Jammu and Kashmir, a single region made up of former kingdoms. The Simla Accord of 1972 stabilized a cease-fire line and gave each of the two nations a section of the disputed land.

Topography

The Republic of Pakistan has three main landscape features. A mountainous region, which is interrupted by deep gorges and narrow passages, is situated along the

The Hindu Kush, Karakoram, and Himalaya ranges meet in northern Pakistan. Together they form a long stretch of peaks where climbers are challenged by the mountainous terrain.

nation's northern frontier. The Indus River divides the southern portion of the nation into two halves, called the Indus River Valley and the Baluchistan Plateau.

Pakistan's rugged northern highlands have long been difficult to travel through and to settle. A chain of mountains called the Hindu Kush runs for several hundred miles in northern Pakistan. The range's highest peak is Tirich Mir, at 25,230 feet above sea level.

The Hindu Kush blends into the Karakoram Range, which Pakistan and India share in the disputed territory of Jammu and Kashmir. The range has about 60 peaks, the tallest of which is K2 (also called Godwin Austen), at 28,250 feet. This mountain lies in Pakistan's section of the territory.

Just south of the Hindu Kush and the Karakoram Range—within the administrative district called the Northern Areas—is

Irrigated valleys, such as this one near Chitral, enable rural inhabitants of northern Pakistan to raise crops.

a small section of the Himalaya Mountains. Nanga Parbat (26,660 feet) is the tallest mountain in Pakistan's portion of the Himalayas, which stretch for 1,500 miles along the northern edge of the Indian sub-continent.

Gaps, or passes, in these mountain chains provide access through the rugged terrain to neighboring countries. The Khyber Pass—located west of the city of Peshawar—provides a route through the Safed Koh Range to Afghanistan.

Similarly, the Baroghil, Kunjerab, and Karakoram passes connect Pakistan to northern Afghanistan and China.

The southern leg of the Indus River divides the rest of Pakistan into two parallel sections. The Indus River Valley, which generally lies east of the waterway, covers most of the provinces of Sind and Punjab and stretches into western India. The Indus has deposited tons of rich soil in the region, making it a fertile agricultural area that covers about 372,000

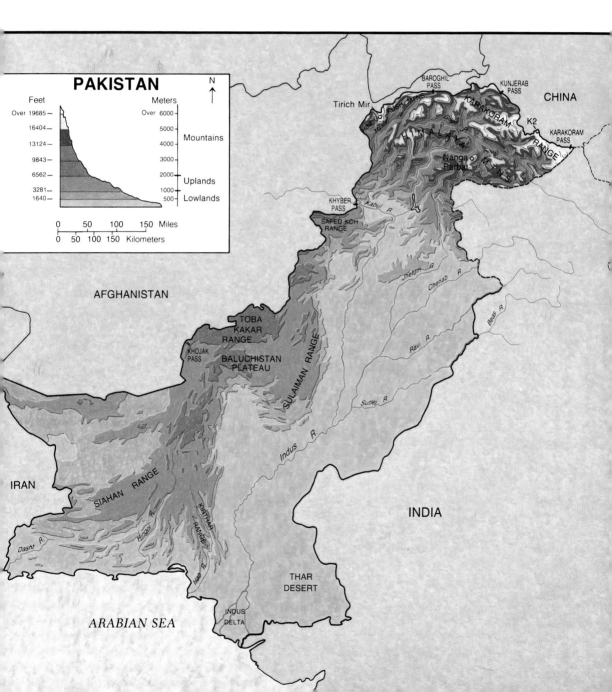

Because the Baluchistan Plateau is largely semi-arid, farmers have difficulty planting and harvesting crops in the region.

square miles. In addition, secondary rivers flow into the Indus, providing further sources of water for crops.

The southeastern portion of the Indus region gradually becomes drier until it blends into the Thar Desert, which lies mostly in western India. The Indus River's delta—a triangular, silt-laden region where the river spreads into several outlets (called mouths) to the sea—appears just southeast of Karachi, the nation's chief port.

The region to the west of the Indus lies mostly in the province of Baluchistan. Dry and sparsely vegetated, the Baluchistan Plateau contains a number of low mountain ranges. The Toba Kakar Range curves along Pakistan's western border, with Khojak Pass providing access to Afghanistan. Along the Indus River is the Sulaiman Range, whose highest peaks exceed 11,000 feet above sea level.

The Siahan and Kirthar ranges fan outward to the southwest and south, respectively, reaching heights of 6,000 to 7,000 feet. Within the Baluchistan Plateau, particularly near the city of Quetta, earthquake tremors occur frequently, although the last massive disturbance was in 1935.

Rivers

Of Pakistan's rivers, the Indus is by far the most important. Intensive farming is possible in eastern sections of the country because of the Indus and other rivers that irrigate the region. The Indus River rises in the Kailas Range of southwestern China, flows west into Pakistan, and turns south in the northern highlands. Its 1,800-mile-long course leads to the Arabian Sea. Small steamers can navigate the river as far as the city of Hyderabad, and the Indus powers hydroelectric facilities at Tarbela.

Several secondary rivers—the Jhelum, Chenab, Ravi, Beas, and Sutlej—travel through Pakistan and eventually join the Indus. Together they empty through the Indus delta into the Arabian Sea. More than 60 percent of the total land under cultivation in Pakistan depends on the vast system of irrigation canals, which draws water from the Indus and its contributing rivers.

The Gilgit River, a northern tributary of the Indus, travels about 150 miles through the Northern Areas. The Kabul begins in Afghanistan and flows east into the Indus at a point that is north of the Khyber Pass. Although generally dry, the Baluchistan Plateau has several small waterways—including the Dasht, Hingol, and Hab rivers—that empty into the Arabian Sea.

Courtesy of Embassy of Pakistan

Trucks and buses wind their way through the Khyber Pass, a narrow gap in the Safed Koh Range that lies between Pakistan and neighboring Afghanistan.

Courtesy of World Bank

The Tarbela Dam harnesses the power of the Indus River— Pakistan's major waterway.

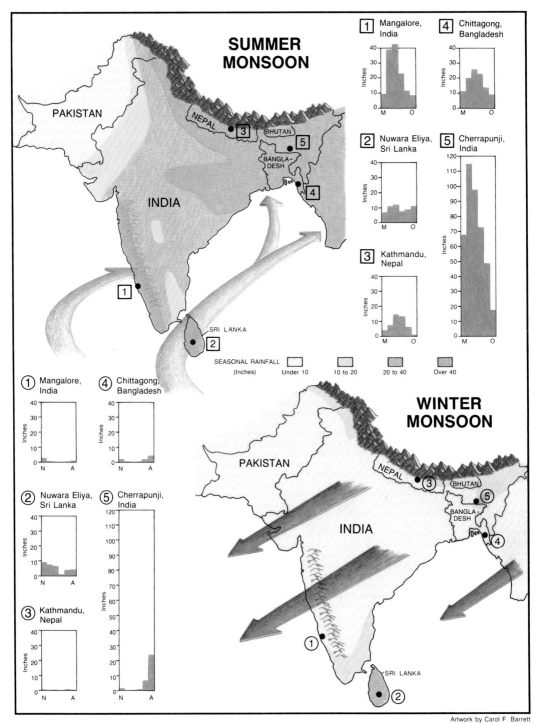

SUMMER MONSOON

PAKISTAN
NEPAL
BHUTAN
BANGLA-DESH
INDIA
SRI LANKA

1 Mangalore, India
4 Chittagong, Bangladesh
2 Nuwara Eliya, Sri Lanka
5 Cherrapunji, India
3 Kathmandu, Nepal

SEASONAL RAINFALL
(Inches)   Under 10   10 to 20   20 to 40   Over 40

WINTER MONSOON

PAKISTAN
NEPAL
BHUTAN
BANGLA-DESH
INDIA
SRI LANKA

Artwork by Carol F. Barrett

These maps show the seasonal shift of winds, called monsoons, over southern Asia and the rainfall levels for five cities in the region. In summer (May to October), the monsoon winds blow from sea to land, carrying moisture – which is released as rain – as they pass over this part of the Asian continent. In winter (November to April), the monsoons blow from land to sea. Because they originate over a cold, arid land surface, the winter winds are dry, and little or no rainfall is associated with them. Although Pakistan is close to the monsoon area of the Indian subcontinent, it does not share the heavy summer rains that typify the west coast of India. Instead, both summer and winter in Pakistan are dry seasons. Climate data taken from *World-Climates* by Willy Rudloff, Stuttgart, 1981.

Climate

Temperatures in the northern mountains average about 75° F in summer (mid-April to mid-July) and below freezing in winter (November to January). Summer is considerably hotter in the Indus region, with temperatures that often rise to 110° F. The sea breezes that cool coastal Karachi most of the year turn hot and dusty in the summer, but the climate generally ranges between 66° and 86° F. Temperatures in Baluchistan average about 80° F in summer and 40° F in winter.

Most of Pakistan's rainfall occurs between July and September, when a seasonal wind, called a monsoon, blows across the country. Pakistan averages only 10 inches of precipitation each year, with Punjab receiving the largest share. Southern areas of the Baluchistan Plateau get the least rainfall—usually less than five inches per year. Despite these general patterns, rainfall can vary greatly from year to year, and Pakistan has experienced both floods and droughts.

Flora and Fauna

Pakistan's plant life varies according to altitude, with higher elevations supporting hardier vegetation, such as firs, pines, junipers, and Himalayan chinars (a Eurasian shade tree). Flowers in the mountains include wild roses and edelweiss, a year-round herb that flourishes at high altitudes.

The Indus region—the scene of much of Pakistan's agricultural activity—has fruit trees, such as mangoes, guavas, and bananas. Cereal grains thrive in the fertile soil, as do walnut trees, grapevines, and berry bushes. In dry or desert regions, sparse grasses or stunted vegetation are most common, although date palms sometimes appear.

Hawks and eagles inhabit the northern mountain zone, where unusual mammals include the Marco Polo sheep, the snow leopard, and the Himalayan black bear. Several varieties of wild goats—such as the markhor and the ibex—also live in the rugged terrain.

Photo by Bill Kish

Among Pakistan's flora are several varieties of wild roses, which generally grow in mountainous regions of the nation.

Vultures – birds of prey that feed on dead animals – abound in Pakistan, where they sometimes gather to devour the carcasses of fallen oxen, goats, and water buffalo.

The plains support herds of deer, goats, sheep, and water buffalo, and the desert regions are home to jackals, hyenas, and camels. Along the coast, the most common forms of wildlife are fish and reptiles that inhabit the Arabian Sea and the delta of the Indus River. Herring, mackerel, and sharks live in the sea, and crocodiles thrive in marshy areas.

Natural Resources

Pakistan exploits few natural resources. Although the production of petroleum has increased sixfold since independence, the nation's total output is still extremely small. In addition to government-sponsored studies, several private companies have also explored for oil.

While searching for oil, scientists discovered large reserves of natural gas in Baluchistan. The gas is used for fuel, fertilizer, and petrochemicals. Low-grade coal deposits are also mined, but production satisfies less than 30 percent of Pakistan's energy requirements.

Although minerals exist in Pakistan, only chromite (from which chrome is made) and bauxite (the raw material for aluminum) are in sufficient supply to make commercial mining profitable. Chromite is exported in substantial amounts. Signifi-

Dromedaries – camels with one hump – dwell in dry areas of Pakistan, where lack of water endangers the survival of other livestock. Frequently moody, camels often whine or spit.

cant deposits of copper, iron ore, manganese, sulfur, gold, and graphite have been discovered. These minerals are difficult to exploit, however, because of their location in Baluchistan, where intense conflicts between the Pakistan army and Baluchi nationalists have occurred in recent times.

Most of Pakistan's minerals are located in Baluchistan, a province that has sometimes been at odds with the national government over the rights to tap the area's natural resources.

Cities

Although most Pakistanis live in villages, in the last two decades, the population has shifted toward major cities. Karachi, with a population of more than five million, is Pakistan's largest city and the capital of Sind province. Once a small fishing village on the Arabian Sea, the city now features many modern buildings and is an important financial hub.

Karachi is also the home of factories that manufacture chemicals, textiles, and glassware and is a shipping outlet for Pakistan's foreign trade. Because of its immense growth since 1947, Karachi faces problems of overcrowding, poor housing, and air pollution. In addition, the arrival

Karachi, the largest city in Pakistan, began as a small fishing village. During the nineteenth century, the British chose Karachi as the capital of Sind, a province of British India. Following independence in 1947, Karachi served as Pakistan's capital until 1965, when the government was moved to Islamabad.

Built in 1634 during the reign of the Mughal emperor Shah Jahan, Wazir Khan Mosque—an Islamic place of prayer—overlooks the city of Lahore in the province of Punjab.

of thousands of refugees who have fled conflicts in Afghanistan has swelled the city's numbers.

About 750 miles northeast of Karachi is Lahore, Pakistan's second largest city, with a population of about three million. Lahore is the nation's cultural center, the site of over 40 colleges and technical institutes, and the capital of Punjab. Records of a settlement at Lahore date back over a thousand years, and the city was an important site for Sikh, Mughal, and British administrations. Among the most important works of the Mughal era is the Shalamar Gardens, which the Mughal emperor Shah Jahan designed in 1642.

Also in Punjab is Rawalpindi (population 928,000). Once the headquarters of regional British administrators, Rawalpindi continues to be the main junction on the route between Peshawar and Lahore. Rawalpindi also served as an interim capital until the new capital—Islamabad—was built.

Begun in 1961, Islamabad (population 200,000) lies at the foot of the mountains of northern Pakistan. By the late 1960s, most government offices had been moved to the new site. A carefully planned urban center, Islamabad blends modern and traditional architectural styles and has distinct governmental, diplomatic, business, and residential zones.

Capital of the North-West Frontier Province, Peshawar (population 555,000) lies near the entrance to the Khyber Pass. As a result, its largely Pathan ethnic population now includes thousands of Afghan refugees who have fled conflicts in their homeland. The refugees, who are also Pathans, generally live in camps surrounding the city. In addition, the exiled leaders of the Afghan resistance movement (the *mujahedeen*) also reside in Peshawar, making the city a focus of mujahedeen activity.

Because of its strategic location, Peshawar was long used as a frontier settlement for Asian trade caravans. The city now manufactures footwear and textiles, processes locally grown food, and trades handicrafts.

Photo by Bernice K. Condit

Buses, bicycles, and horse-drawn vehicles crisscross an intersection in Rawalpindi, which lies within a few miles of Islamabad—Pakistan's capital city.

Courtesy of UNHCR

The arrival in the 1980s of millions of Afghan refugees to urban and rural areas of Pakistan put pressure on the nation's housing and food resources.

The earliest records of settlements in Pakistan are based on findings within the ruined cities of Mohenjo-Daro and Harappa. Excavations of Mohenjo-Daro uncovered many small statues, including an animal's head *(left)* and the figure of a priest or king *(right)*.

2) History and Government

Because Pakistan and India share ethnic and cultural backgrounds, the early history of what is now Pakistan is also the history of India. Archaeological findings, including cave paintings and stone tools, indicate that ancestors of the human family first settled on the subcontinent 400,000 years ago. These humanoids hunted and gathered their food. Much later, about 4000 B.C., another culture emerged, and its people lived in permanent villages and used more complex tools.

Indus Civilization

Scientists believe that large-scale settlements in Pakistan began about 2500 B.C. along the fertile banks of the Indus River and its many tributaries. A complex urban civilization grew in this region and, at its peak, included western India.

Archaeologists have uncovered over 300 well-designed cities that featured unique architectural styles. The two main urban centers were Mohenjo-Daro, in what is now Sind, and Harappa, in present-day Punjab.

The city of Mohenjo-Daro consisted of red brick structures in square or rectangular groupings. Streets were often wide and were sometimes paved, and buildings included public administration centers, religious colleges, royal palaces, and communal granaries (shared storage places for food). Excavations have uncovered about 250 acres of Mohenjo-Daro, although outer parts of this urban center are still buried.

Above this carving of a bull are writing symbols from the Indus civilization. Language experts have yet to interpret these characters.

Harappa—the first of the Indus cities to be discovered—is smaller and not as well preserved as Mohenjo-Daro is. The economy of Harappa depended on trade and farming, and its buildings included a fortress and a granary.

The Indus civilization standardized weights and measures and produced surplus crops to trade. The cities had extensive drainage systems, well-defined neighborhoods, and protected administrative headquarters. A system of picture

The ruins of Mohenjo-Daro cover about 250 acres in Sind province. Some historians suggest that the Indus civilization declined in about 1800 B.C. as a result of invasion by a central Asian people called Aryans.

writing existed, but modern experts have yet to decipher it. Natural environmental factors (such as flooding), overpopulation, or invasion may have caused the Indus civilization to decline in about 1800 B.C.

ARYANS

Arriving from central Asia between 2000 and 1000 B.C., a people called Aryans (or Indo-Aryans) conquered and ruled northern regions of the subcontinent. The Aryans developed a philosophy that evolved into the Hindu religion. Their highly structured framework included a caste system, under which citizens became members of rigid social and professional groups. In addition to spreading their philosophy, the Aryans brought iron tools, the horse and chariot, and knowledge of astronomy and mathematics to the region.

Sixteen political units arose in the Aryan territory during the next 1,000 years. The realms stretched across the northern subcontinent from modern Afghanistan to Bangladesh. In present-day Pakistan, the Aryans developed settlements that served the trade caravans passing through the region.

Magadha, Gandhara, and Kushan

By about the middle of the sixth century B.C., Magadha had emerged as the most powerful Indo-Aryan state. Its rise was accompanied by religious reform movements that resulted in the founding of Buddhism and Jainism, both of which were religious offshoots of Hinduism. Magadha's location —in northeastern India at the crossroads of major trade routes—and its access to rich soil and iron deposits helped to make it a stable kingdom.

At roughly the same time as Magadha's rise to power, northern Pakistan came

A pre-Islamic Hindu sculpture—suggestive of Pakistan's varied religious past—bears the ravages of the area's weather.

The philosophy of the Aryans developed into the Hindu religion. Here, Siva (also known as the Destroyer), one of Hinduism's main gods, is depicted dancing within a circle. The god is said to destroy life in order to create it.

under the authority of the Gandhara kingdom, which was centered near present-day Peshawar. West of Gandhara was the realm of Alexander the Great of Greece, who was pushing toward the Indus River through the regions now known as Afghanistan and Iran. Gandhara, therefore, was caught between two expanding and aggressive kingdoms.

Arriving by way of the Khyber Pass and the Kabul River Valley, Alexander invaded Gandhara in 327 B.C. and defeated the forces of the Gandhara king Porus. Alexander's troops—who had been fighting for nearly a decade—threatened to mutiny if

A bust of Alexander the Great shows him at the height of his military conquests. In the fourth century B.C. Alexander and his Greek troops defeated the armies of Porus, king of Gandhara.

21

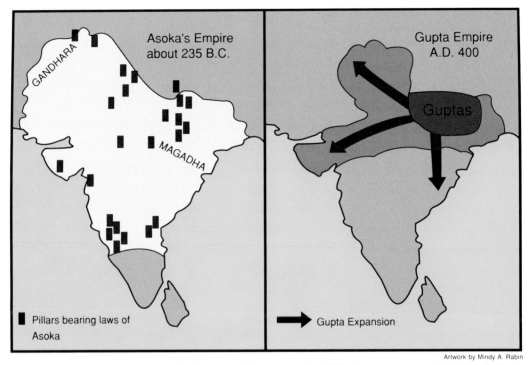

Asoka's Empire
about 235 B.C.

GANDHARA

MAGADHA

■ Pillars bearing laws of
Asoka

Gupta Empire
A.D. 400

Guptas

➤ Gupta Expansion

Artwork by Mindy A. Rabin

The empire *(left)* of the Mauryan leader Asoka stretched from present-day Afghanistan to eastern and southern India. By about A.D. 400 the Gupta Empire *(right)* had established a foothold in the western Kushan Empire, which covered much of Pakistan.

their leader did not turn homeward. Alexander led his soldiers south along the Indus River, and they sailed for Greece in about 324 B.C.

The Magadha leader Candragupta Maurya expanded his holdings westward, conquering Gandhara soon after Alexander's departure. He founded the Maurya dynasty (family of rulers), which governed all of Pakistan and much of India for about a century. The most famous of the Maurya rulers was Candragupta's grandson Asoka, who reigned from 273 to 232 B.C. He made Buddhism the official religion of his realm and encouraged the construction of many massive Buddhist buildings.

The strong Buddhist belief in nonviolence caused Asoka to reject force as a means of governing. His laws—carved on huge pillars—focused on moral and social duties and included themes of tolerance and harmony. Yet Asoka—not his prin-

ciples—had become the center of the realm, and within a century of his death in 232 B.C., the empire shrank back to within the original borders of Magadha.

After Maurya disintegrated, Gandhara flourished as a cultural center within the Kushan Empire. The Kushan, who came from the Hindu Kush, developed Perushapure (near Peshawar) as their capital and ruled between A.D. 50 and about A.D. 250. Their territory included areas of modern Afghanistan, China, the former Soviet Union, Pakistan, and India.

Like Asoka, the Kushan king Kaniska adopted the Buddhist faith. In keeping with Buddhist beliefs, he tolerated other religions, especially Hinduism.

Kushan's economy depended on peaceful trade. By the first century A.D., the Kushan controlled sections of caravan routes, including the Silk Road, which linked the Persian, Chinese, and Roman empires.

Guptas, Ephthalites, and Rajputs

In the fourth century, the Gupta Empire, which was centered in eastern India, expanded and eventually absorbed the western Kushan Empire, including Pakistan. The Guptas, a Hindu people, made discoveries in mathematics, astronomy, and the arts. Scholars compiled dictionaries of the Sanskrit language, which was in use at the time, and mathematicians calculated the shape and movement of the planets.

In the fifth century, Ephthalites (also called White Huns)—a people from central Asia—crossed into the northern regions of the Kushan Empire and conquered its people. The Ephthalites also attacked the Guptas and substantially weakened their empire. The invaders destroyed Hindu and Buddhist temples in Punjab and headed east to India, where an alliance of princedoms defeated them in the mid-sixth century.

By the seventh century, Hindu and Buddhist dynasties throughout the subcontinent were competing for former Gupta territory. Many of these rivals were based in Punjab and belonged to the Hindu Rajput clan, whose soldiers were famous for their aggressive and skillful military tactics.

Rajput rulers protected their lands in Punjab from outsiders but did little to develop them internally. As a result, trade declined, and outdated farming techniques remained in use. Their isolation also made the Rajputs unaware of outside events. One of these events was the rise of Islam, a monotheistic (one-god) religion founded in the seventh century by the prophet Muhammad in what is now Saudi Arabia. The new faith urged believers to expand their territory and to convert conquered peoples to Islam.

Muslim Rule

Muslims—followers of the Islamic religion —gained control of what is now Pakistan

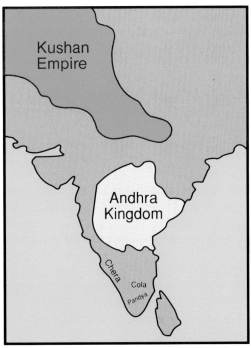

Artwork by Mindy A. Rabin

The Kushan Empire was located at the commercial crossroads of central Asia and depended heavily on trade to survive.

Museum of Fine Arts, Boston

By the seventh century, Rajput princes controlled much of the northwestern subcontinent, including parts of what is now Pakistan.

23

through a series of military and cultural conquests over five centuries. Muslim sailors from Arabia first landed on the shores of Sind soon after the death of Muhammad in A.D. 632. Migrations of newly converted Arab traders followed, and these merchants brought their faith with them as they conducted business along the coast of the Arabian Sea.

Sufis (Islamic mystics) also played a role in the spread of Islam to south central Asia. The people of the Punjab and Sind regions of Pakistan responded well to the simple lifestyles of these religious people. Many Hindus at the bottom of the caste system converted to the new religion, which, unlike Hinduism, did not include social divisions. The arrival of Islamic Turks and Afghans, who moved from the west and who settled in Pakistan and India, also spread Islam.

The tombs at Chaukundi, near Karachi, date from the thirteenth to the sixteenth centuries, when the Delhi sultanate (kingdom) ruled regions in modern Pakistan.

Muslim attacks on Pakistan began in earnest under Mahmud of Ghazna, who ruled a region now shared by Afghanistan and Iran from 999 to 1030. In the early eleventh century Mahmud began to raid the Rajput kingdoms. Initially, Mahmud sought the wealth of the area. His troops sacked richly decorated Hindu temples for treasures to take back to his realm. In time, however, Mahmud desired a local base from which to stage his raids. By 1025 he had added Punjab to his empire.

Muhammad Ghuri completed the Muslim conquest of the subcontinent in the late twelfth century. He established his capital at Delhi, India, and went on to subdue northern regions between modern Pakistan and present-day Bangladesh. His armies overthrew the Rajputs, and the new Islamic government discontinued the caste system. Several casteless religions emerged, including Sikhism, which arose in Punjab and which combined elements of both Hinduism and Islam.

DELHI SULTANATE

Five dynasties of the Delhi sultanate (kingdom) ruled throughout the period of Muslim control in Pakistan and India, and each came to power by using violence. Muhammad Ghuri's successor, the former slave Qutb-ud-Din Aybak, was the first ruler of the Slave dynasty, which lasted from 1206 to 1290. Later dynasties of the Delhi sultanate—the Khalji, the Tughluq, the Sayyid, and the Lodi—consolidated their control over Pakistan and northern India between 1260 and 1526.

Clashes between Muslims and subject Hindu populations often occurred during the 320-year rule of the Delhi sultanate. Occasionally, the two cultures blended successfully. Periods of harmony produced the Quwwat-ul-Islam Mosque (Muslim place of prayer) in Delhi and a variety of Hindu-Muslim musical compositions that became popular throughout the subcontinent. At other times, however, religious intolerance motivated Muslims to destroy

The city of Thatta was the capital of Sind during the Mughal era. Just outside the city is a vast collection of above-ground burial sites for important members of the Mughal administration.

Hindu temples, resulting in distrust between the two groups.

The Delhi sultanate slowly declined after 1398, when the Mongol conqueror Timur the Lame (also known as Tamerlane) swept down from central Asia and sacked Delhi. The Delhi sultanate survived for only one more century before falling in 1526 to Zahir-ud-Din Muhammad, a descendant of Timur.

Mughal Empire

Zahir-ud-Din Muhammad, who was called Babur by his followers, united northern India and Pakistan under his rule between 1526 and 1530 and laid the foundations of the Mughal Empire. (Mughal is derived from the word *Mongol.*) The new leaders were talented administrators, skilled military strategists, and able diplomats in foreign and domestic affairs. The empire

Akbar, a sixteenth-century Mughal emperor, built Lahore Fort. His successors, Jahangir and Shah Jahan, substantially improved the original structure, which was designed to be a royal palace.

A miniature painting from the Mughal period shows the emperor in conference with his advisers.

traded heavily and generated immense wealth. In addition, its policy of religious tolerance calmed the Hindus, who had feared that Islamic Mughals would try to convert them.

The Mughal realm grew larger through marriage connections and through contracts with smaller Hindu and Muslim princedoms—rarely through military conquest. At its height, the empire governed Pakistan and nearly all of India.

The Mughal Empire flourished under Babur's grandson Akbar, who reigned from 1556 to 1605. The emperor cultivated the goodwill of the Hindus, especially of the Rajputs, by placing some of them in high positions in his government. To strengthen the bond between the two cultures, Akbar encouraged intermarriage between Rajputs and Muslims.

Akbar's immediate successors, first Jahangir and then Shah Jahan, were able to hold the empire together with little effort, partly because of the strong organization that Akbar had left behind. They also followed the policy of religious tolerance begun by the Mughals. During the reign of Shah Jahan, Islamic architecture reached an artistic peak that is best exemplified by the Taj Mahal in Agra (north central India) and by the Shalamar Gardens in Lahore, Pakistan.

Shah Jahan's son, Alamgir (also called Aurangzeb), forced his father to leave the throne in 1658. A strict Muslim, the new emperor attempted to return to traditional Islamic ways and to expand his empire. He harassed Hindus by destroying their temples and by taxing them heavily. After the death of Alamgir in 1707, the Mughal Empire began to collapse as smaller realms rebelled against the central government.

Trade with Europe

Europeans had traded with Pakistan and India in ancient times. They renewed their contact in 1498, when the Portuguese navigator Vasco da Gama visited the subcontinent. The Portuguese established commercial links and brought Mughal goods to Europe throughout the sixteenth century. Reports of the wealth of the Mughal Empire stirred Britain, France, and the Netherlands to compete with Portugal for the empire's trade.

In the seventeenth century, with the permission of the Mughal emperor Jahangir, the British East India Company established several commercial outposts on the Indian subcontinent. Surat, now in the Indian state of Gujarat, became the firm's main northwestern port. The French also managed to get a share of the Indian trade, claiming Pondichéry in southern India in 1670. The subcontinent's relationship with Europe was mostly commercial, and Mughal emperors and the trading companies

In 1634 the governor of Punjab, Wazir Khan, sponsored the construction of a mosque. Called Wazir Khan Mosque, the building features beautiful tilework in intricate geometric patterns.

Courtesy of Nathan Rabe

27

A page from a seventeenth-century album depicts the Mughal emperor Shah Jahan. During his reign (1628–1658), Mughal architecture reached an artistic height exemplified by the Shalamar Gardens, which the emperor designed in 1642.

profited from the exchange of spices and textiles.

BRITISH EXPANSION AND THE SIKH KINGDOM

The stability of the Mughal Empire and the commercial situation changed suddenly at the beginning of the eighteenth century. Following the death of Alamgir, regional rivalries within and between Hindu and Muslim states erupted all over Pakistan and India. These conflicts eventually allowed the British and the French to take control of the subcontinent's valuable trade.

Fearful of losing their commercial arrangements, Britain and France each made alliances with princedoms in order to expel the other European power from the subcontinent. In this way the British absorbed the western princedoms of Sind, Hyderabad, and Khairpur in the 1830s. Britain also gained authority over Baluchistan by treaty in 1854.

The princes, in turn, took advantage of the rivalry between the British and the French to gain power over other local rulers. For example, the Sikhs—a religious community that had formed an independent realm—took over kingdoms in Kashmir and Peshawar. Under their leader, Maharaja (prince) Ranjit Singh, the Sikhs developed a strong administration that was centered in Lahore.

After Ranjit Singh's death in 1839, quarrels arose over the division of his lands among his successors. Traditionally, lands to the east of the Sutlej River had been regarded as under British control. After the maharaja's death, however, his successors sought to expand their holdings to include those of the British. Sikh fighters and British troops clashed in 1845, and

Called the Lion of the Punjab, Ranjit Singh succeeded his father in 1792 as head of the Sikh confederacy. After seizing lands in what is now Pakistan, he and his troops clashed with the British over territorial goals in the 1840s.

the Europeans defeated their opponents in 1846. A second Sikh defeat in 1849 brought Punjab completely under British rule.

British Rule

For the next 100 years, Britain steadily extended its influence, and, by the middle of the nineteenth century, it had firm control over nearly the entire subcontinent. The expansion and protection of Britain's trade—as well as a desire to secure colonial territory against foreign or local threats—motivated the British to take power in both Pakistan and India. In addition, Britain felt that it should spread European culture—social ideas and Christianity in particular—throughout its colonial holdings.

The British East India Company continued to exercise political power without the direct involvement of the British government until 1858. Between 1857 and 1858, rebellions erupted in eastern and central India. Among the many causes of the revolts was the Indians' fear of British efforts to convert both Muslims and Hindus to Christianity.

Fighting continued for 10 months, until British troops defeated the rebels. As a result of the conflicts, Britain transferred responsibility for India from the East India Company to the British Crown. The British then adopted two policies to ensure that they would have strong control over the subcontinent. Britain promised not to interfere in the religious affairs of the people, and it gathered the support of local leaders for its colonial administration.

Courtesy of National Army Museum, London

A drawing illustrates the Battle of Sobraon in 1846 during a war between the Sikhs *(in white turbans)*—**who controlled Lahore, Kashmir, Peshawar, and Multan—and the British.**

29

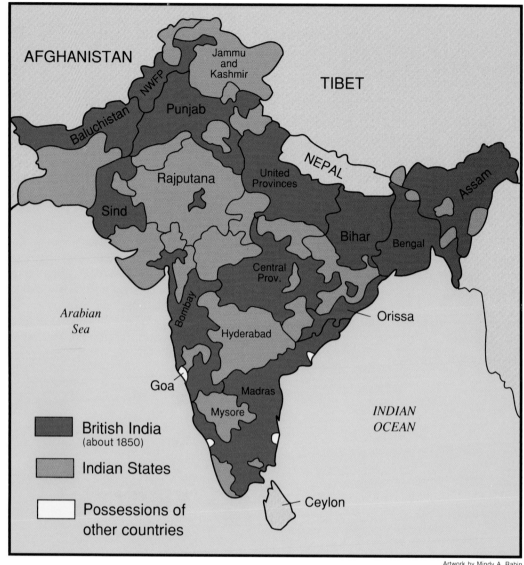

Artwork by Mindy A. Rabin

"British India" consisted of provinces—such as Punjab and most of Sind—that the British directly administered. Princes ruled independent states, which included part of Baluchistan and the North-West Frontier Province (NWFP), according to treaties the princes had made with the British.

BRITISH INDIA

The term "British India" refers to the region of the subcontinent that was under direct British authority. A resident official of the British government, usually the governor-general, indirectly controlled the princely states—territories that were under British military protection but were ruled by local princes. The governor-general held executive and legislative authority, with district officers handling local administrative matters.

In the northwestern regions of the subcontinent, the holdings of British India included Sind, Punjab, and parts of what came to be called the North-West Frontier Province (NWFP). Baluchistan, Gilgit, and Jammu and Kashmir were princely states.

The British built extensive railway, road, and telegraph networks, extended irrigation systems in the Indus Valley, and distributed food during famines. Britain relied on the subcontinent as a source of raw materials and as a market for British-manufactured goods. Colonial administrators, however, made little effort to keep the region economically independent. As a result, the subcontinent's formerly self-sufficient economy became tied to markets over which it had no control.

Opposition to British Rule

Opposition to British rule emerged slowly, beginning with the formation of the Indian National Congress in 1885. The original aim of the congress was self-rule —but not total independence—for India within the British Empire. Over several decades, the congress, whose members were mostly Hindus, became the only organization that had widespread national support.

Muslims formed the second largest group in India's population, but they were greatly outnumbered by Hindus. The British supported the creation of the All-India Muslim League in 1906 as a counterbalance to the Indian National Congress.

Mohammed Ali Jinnah—whom Pakistanis call Quaid-i-Azam, or Great Leader —headed the league. Under his leadership, it grew from a small, weak group splintered by internal disagreements into an influential political party. Jinnah strongly advocated Hindu-Muslim cooperation. Like Mohandas K. Gandhi—who headed the Indian National Congress—Jinnah supported a united, independent Indian state.

Social barriers that had formed under the British led to the creation of nationalist organizations and opposition movements. Ethnic discrimination became common in colonial India. In the Indian army, only the British served as officers. In addition, the British designated certain groups—Sikhs and Pathans (people from the NWFP), for example—as naturally suited to military pursuits. The British

recruited large numbers of soldiers from these ethnic communities.

While the Hindu population sought a single voice with which to address the colonial regime, the Muslim population also struggled for unity. In general, however, Muslim efforts were more disjointed than those of Hindus.

One area in which Muslims were very active was education. In the last quarter of the nineteenth century, ulama (Islamic scholars) led the Deoband movement, which tried to reinterpret Muslim teachings for contemporary society. Similarly, the Aligarh movement in northern India encouraged Muslims to move up in the colonial social and political ranks by obtaining a British-style, yet Islamic, education. The movement's center—Aligarh College—cultivated ethnic loyalty to Britain within an Islamic religious context.

Called Quaid-i-Azam (Great Leader), Mohammed Ali Jinnah became president of the Muslim League in 1913. By the 1930s he viewed a divided India–between Muslims and Hindus–as the only solution to economic and religious inequality.

World War I and Its Aftermath

More than one million soldiers from the subcontinent fought with British troops in Europe and the Middle East during World War I (1914–1918). Nationalist leaders co-operated with Britain, in part because they expected that Britain would give them greater postwar involvement in the government. The Government of India Act of 1919, however, made few changes and did not satisfy India's Muslim or Hindu leaders.

The Indian National Congress continued to attract millions of Indians and developed a Pan-Indian approach to politics —that is, it sought to unite religious, language, and ethnic groups. But Jinnah and other Muslim activists, such as Muhammad Iqbal, grew more disillusioned with the congress's policies. These leaders became convinced that Muslims would never be guaranteed their rights in a united India that was predominantly Hindu.

Jinnah announced a plan in 1929 for a separate Muslim voter roll and guaranteed representation for Muslims in any future independent Indian government. In 1930 Iqbal outlined the concept of a federated India, in which a separate Muslim state— made up of Punjab, the NWFP, Sind, and Baluchistan—would exist.

After negotiating with various Indian leaders, Britain passed a new Government of India Act in 1935. The plan had two goals. It sought to satisfy the demands of Hindus and Muslims for self-rule and to unite the states of the subcontinent into a single nation. Many princes objected to the plan because they felt that the new act weakened their power. Although princely resistance made it impossible to carry out the part of the plan calling for unification, the new legislation established independent provincial governments. The Indian National Congress dominated most of these regional councils.

Encouraged by the British colonial administration, Sikhs and Pathans became members of military units within the British army and fought in both world wars.

Road to Independence

At the outset of World War II (1939–1945), Britain declared itself and its empire, including India, to be at war with Germany. Because Britain had not involved the Indian National Congress in making this decision, the congress refused to cooperate with Britain during the global conflict. The Muslim League, on the other hand, supported Britain during the war in the hope of gaining postwar support for the rights of the Muslim community. They especially wanted to establish a separate Muslim nation to be called Pakistan—a name formed from the first letters of regions in the northwest.

The Muslim League passed a declaration of independence, called the Lahore Resolution, on March 23, 1940. (That day is now a national holiday called Pakistan Day.) The resolution declared that the British and Indian governments should form independent states of the areas in which the Muslims comprised a majority. The document referred specifically to zones in northwestern and eastern India. The league also rejected the idea of a federated India and argued that Partition (the division of India into Hindu and Muslim territories) was the only way to ensure Muslim social, political, and economic equality.

After World War II ended, the British —who saw the inevitability of independence for India—tried to find common ground between the Indian National Congress and the Muslim League. But the split between the two groups was so great that agreement on a postindependence government proved impossible to reach. The British also began to view Partition as the only solution.

Despite the fact that Indian Muslims had a common goal in wanting to form a separate state, they were motivated to support Partition for a variety of reasons. In the fertile northwestern regions, the Muslim population—which included many wealthy landholders—sought religious authority and security. The Muslims of north

Photo by UPI/Bettmann Newsphotos

At a gathering of the Muslim League in 1943—four years before Pakistan was established—Jinnah *(at the podium)* **addressed a crowd of supporters about the need for a separate nation for India's Muslim population.**

central India—surrounded geographically by Hindu-dominated provinces—wanted to be free of Hindu control. The Muslims of Bengal and Assam—parts of which would later become East Pakistan—desired reforms in the distribution of land and economic opportunity. They believed that these reforms could be achieved only through an independent nation.

Partition and Independence

In June 1947, Britain announced a plan to establish two nations from its holdings on the subcontinent. India would have a Hindu majority and Pakistan, a Muslim majority. The main religious group in a given region would determine to which new nation the territory would belong. Muslims of the northwestern regions chose to form

33

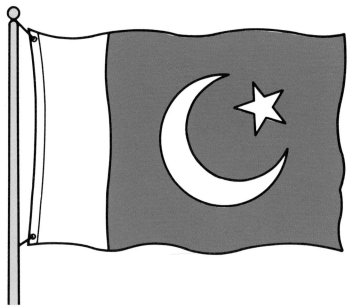

The Muslim League adopted the Islamic symbols of a crescent and star on a field of green as its emblem in 1906. The white stripe was added at independence in 1947 to represent the religious minorities within the new nation of Pakistan.

Artwork by Laura Westlund

West Pakistan, and Muslims of East Bengal made up East Pakistan. More than 1,000 miles of Indian territory separated the two wings of the new nation. The British plan allowed the princely states to join either India or Pakistan or to remain independent.

The Congress party and the Muslim League agreed to the plan, despite its difficulties. In August 1947, Britain formally acknowledged that India and Pakistan were independent. Both became dominions within the British Commonwealth—that is, self-governing nations that acknowledged the British monarch as their symbolic head.

Bloody rioting accompanied Partition, particularly in Punjab, as over 10 million people tried to move across the new boundaries to the country of their choice. Estimates indicate that 500,000 Muslims died as their new nation was taking shape. West Pakistan lost its Hindu and Sikh populations, which had controlled much of the region's commercial network. Muslim immigrants, called muhajirs, moved from their birthplaces in central India, in East Punjab, or in West Bengal to either wing of the new Muslim nation.

East Pakistan also had economic problems. Long the site of India's jute industry, Bengal became divided between the growers and the manufacturers of jute (a fiber used in rope making). Jute farms lay in East Pakistan, but the factories that made jute products were located in the Indian state of West Bengal. As a result, the Bengali Muslims of East Pakistan lost access to the markets for their crop and lacked the industrial machinery needed to provide substitute outlets.

Despite these setbacks, the government of the Dominion of Pakistan established itself in Karachi, the nation's first capital city. Mohammed Ali Jinnah became the first governor-general of Pakistan, and Liaquat Ali Khan served as his prime minister. Jinnah's popularity allowed him to combine the offices of head of state, leader of the Muslim League, and governor-general into one office.

Early Challenges

The princely state of Jammu and Kashmir had been a predominantly Muslim realm ruled by a Hindu prince. After Partition, the princedom refused to join either India or Pakistan. The government of Pakistan believed that the majority Muslim population should become part of a Muslim—and not a Hindu—nation.

Muslim militants from the NWFP caused disturbances in Jammu and Kashmir. The region's Hindu leader thereupon agreed to join the Indian union in return for military assistance to repel the Pakistanis. Indian troops entered the area and clashes resulted. India claimed the entire region, but Pakistan refused to accept the prince's pro-Indian decision. The United Nations (UN) established a cease-fire line that snaked through Jammu and Kashmir. Despite continued conflicts, the division has remained intact since 1949.

In September 1948 Jinnah died, and Khwaja Nazimuddin of East Pakistan succeeded him as governor-general. The additional offices that Jinnah had held were given to other politicians. Political instability followed Jinnah's death and brought about frequent party realignments and cabinet changes. The holders of the various top offices tried to limit each other's power, with the greatest tension occurring between Governor-general Nazimuddin and Prime Minister Liaquat.

Political leaders could not agree about what it meant to be a Muslim nation. Thus, the people continued to think of themselves as Bengalis, Punjabis, and Sindhi instead of as Pakistanis. In October 1951, Liaquat was assassinated, and, within the next seven years, Pakistan had six prime ministers. With no leaders of Jinnah's or Liaquat's stature to unite the country, Pakistan could not achieve the kind of internal stability that was necessary for progress. Internationally, Pakistan allied itself with the U.S. and Europe by joining regional defense organizations such as SEATO and CENTO, thereby gaining U.S. and other foreign aid.

A Bloodless Revolution

In the late 1940s, an assembly had been formed to write a constitution that would be acceptable to the two wings of Pakistan. Sharp divisions within the country became evident as years passed without a written document that declared the

Jute—a fibrous plant that these Bengali farmers are harvesting—became a source of tension between East and West Pakistan (the two wings of the newly formed nation of Pakistan). East Pakistan, where jute farms were located, lost access to processing factories in India after independence. Without the means to process the crop, East Pakistan sent its jute to more-industrialized West Pakistan. As a result, much of the revenue from jute exports funded projects in West Pakistan.

Courtesy of Embassy of Bangladesh

Until 1965, when Pakistan's leader Mohammad Ayub Khan moved the nation's capital to Islamabad, the legislature met in Karachi.

nation's ideas and goals. Finally, in 1956 the assembly produced a constitution that changed Pakistan from a dominion to an Islamic republic.

But the various emerging political parties—including the Republican party, the Awami League, and the United Front—disagreed about the constitution's election rules and about the distribution of power. The republic's first president, Iskander Mirza, suspended the new constitution and ousted the prime minister, H. S. Suhrawardy. Regional violence erupted in Baluchistan, the NWFP, and East Pakistan. The economy declined during this period of disruption, and Pakistanis lost confidence in their government.

In 1958 a group of senior military officers took control of the nation's affairs. On October 7, President Mirza, General Mohammad Ayub Khan, and other senior officers proclaimed a bloodless revolution. The president declared martial law (rule by the military) and dismissed both the central and provincial governments. Within three weeks of the coup, however, the military exiled Mirza to Great Britain. General Ayub Khan named himself chief martial law administrator and became a military dictator.

The Ayub Khan Era

After the coup of 1958, General Ayub Khan's administration brought many changes. Politicians and bureaucrats convicted of corruption were dismissed, and people who supported the general took their place. Ayub Khan enacted a land reform plan that limited each landowner to no more than 500 acres of irrigated land or 1,000 acres of unirrigated land. Changes in the laws granted equal rights to women, including the right to run for government office.

The new regime built many schools to combat the problem of illiteracy, and it designed other projects to improve health standards, industry, defense, and communications. Rawalpindi (the headquarters of the army) temporarily replaced Karachi as the capital of Pakistan until the new capital in Islamabad—a few miles from Rawalpindi—was completed.

Changes in the economic structure, as well as loans from more developed countries, spurred growth and development in agricultural and technical fields. Yet the government controlled the unions, and most laborers continued to live in poverty. Press censorship limited information about the government's activities.

The 1960s

The 1960s saw a deterioration in Pakistan's relations with Afghanistan, principally over their mutual border. The Pathan-dominated Afghan government had long supported fellow Pathans in the NWFP and had pushed for an independent state—to be called Pakthunistan—for Pakistan's Pathans.

Efforts to disturb the government of the NWFP soured relations between Ayub Khan and Sardar Mohammad Daud Khan,

Independent Picture Service

Trained in the British army, in which he served between 1928 and 1947, Ayub Khan enacted political and economic reforms after coming to power in 1958.

who was then prime minister of Afghanistan. The countries broke diplomatic relations in 1961 and closed the borders to one another's trade. (The dispute has caused less friction between the two countries since 1980, when conflicts in Afghanistan turned that nation's attention toward its internal problems.)

In 1962 a committee drafted a new constitution. The document gave the president more control over the legislature, the power to plan the budget, and the authority to suspend basic rights during national emergencies. In addition, the constitution arranged for members of local councils—called Basic Democracies—to elect the president for the general population. Soon after the constitution took effect, Ayub Khan suspended martial law, allowed political parties to function, and scheduled new elections for 1965.

After the 1965 elections, a majority of Basic Democrats chose Ayub Khan as president over Fatima Jinnah, the sister of Mohammed Ali Jinnah. Opposition parties objected to the government's control of the press, and they felt that the constitution was wrong in allowing the president to veto, ignore, or initiate legislation.

By 1968 internal opposition to Ayub Khan had grown. Foreign minister Zulfikar Ali Bhutto resigned his post to organize the Pakistan People's party (PPP). Even members of the military—Ayub Khan's traditional supporters—began to express discontent. The president's poor health also contributed to his loss of political control.

Rise of Bengali Nationalism

In 1969 another military coup—this time carried out by Mohammad Yahya Khan, commander-in chief of the army—forced Ayub Khan's resignation. Yahya Khan suspended the 1962 constitution and became head of a new regime of martial law. Eventually, Yahya Khan named himself president.

37

The president scheduled elections for November of 1970. The date was postponed to December 1970, however, because a severe cyclone hit East Pakistan in November. The disaster claimed more than one million lives and caused massive damage. East Pakistanis felt that the central government was slow to respond to their plight. Indeed, help from international relief agencies came in before aid arrived from West Pakistan.

Aside from a common religion, the Bengalis of East Pakistan had little connection to Pakistanis in the western half of the nation. Perhaps the most important conflict between the two wings arose because East Pakistan felt economically exploited by West Pakistan, particularly by the dominant Punjabi population.

East Pakistan provided the country with jute—the nation's chief export and cash crop. The government built mills to process the jute, which was then exported overseas. The income earned from jute products was not funneled back into East Pakistan but instead went to the industrial sector in West Pakistan. These concerns, along with the government's slow response to the cyclone, heightened tensions during the 1970 elections.

Birth of Bangladesh

The 1970 elections, which would determine who would be prime minister, brought two opposing ideas and political personalities to the public's attention. In West Pakistan, Bhutto and his PPP won a majority of votes, while Mujibur Rahman (called Mujib) and the Awami League overwhelmingly dominated East Pakistan. Bhutto advocated economic reforms and centralized authority, while Mujib wanted more self-rule for East Pakistan.

Successful government would depend on Bhutto, Mujib, and Yahya Khan being able to work together. Bhutto boycotted the convening of the legislature, and, as a result, Yahya Khan postponed the first meeting. Mujib set down the conditions under which he would participate in the government—as prime minister and as head of the majority party in the assembly. These conditions were unacceptable to Bhutto and the president. Bhutto had Mujib arrested and taken to West Pakistan.

Workers unload a sack of rice from China following the disastrous cyclone of November 1970 that devastated much of East Pakistan.

UPI/Bettmann Newsphotos

A member of the Bengali *Mukti Bahini* (Liberation Army) joins in a rebel advance on the city of Jessore in East Pakistan. East Pakistanis and Indian forces fought troops of West Pakistan throughout 1971. The conflict ended when East Pakistan declared its independence and formed a new nation called Bangladesh.

Mujib's supporters fled to India, where they set up a government-in-exile for the proposed independent Bengali nation of Bangladesh.

Between March and December of 1971, troops of Pakistan's army clashed with members of the Bengali *Mukti Bahini* (Liberation Army). By late 1971, estimates indicated that nearly eight million East Pakistanis had fled the conflict by crossing the border into India. Violence, famine, and epidemic diseases threatened those who remained.

Pakistan conducted air raids into India's territory in search of guerrilla fighters. In response, Indian forces fought alongside the Bengalis, taking Dacca—the main city in East Pakistan—in December 1971. In-

dia recognized the provisional government of the new nation of Bangladesh on December 6, and Pakistan's army surrendered on December 16. Twenty-four hours later, India's prime minister, Indira Gandhi, called a cease-fire, and Yahya Khan resigned.

Bhutto and Zia

Following the loss of its eastern wing through a decisive military defeat, the government in West Pakistan asked Bhutto to rule what remained of Pakistan. Bhutto sought to lead the nation away from its dependence on the United States and established friendly contacts with the Soviet Union and several Arab states. Bhutto and Indira Gandhi signed the Simla Accord, which provided for the return from India of 90,000 prisoners of war. In exchange, Bhutto assured India that Pakistan would not attempt to take the state of Jammu and Kashmir by force.

After 13 years under military rule, the people of Pakistan wanted Bhutto to improve economic and social conditions. Bhutto promised land reform, and he nationalized (changed from private to government ownership) much of the industrial sector. In general, he was able to revive the nearly collapsed economy that he had inherited in 1971. He also aimed to make Pakistan a one-party state. To achieve this goal, he needed a landslide victory in a general election, an event that would demonstrate the PPP's countrywide popularity.

Bhutto held elections in 1977, manipulating the results to assure the victory of his party. This action led to widespread public discontent, and riots broke out. Bhutto declared martial law in Lahore, Karachi, and Hyderabad. In July 1977, the situation went out of control. The army seized power and jailed Bhutto. The new government accused the former prime minister of involvement in the attempted murder of a PPP politician. Bhutto was tried, was found guilty, and was executed in April

1979. Meanwhile, General Mohammed Zia ul-Haq proclaimed himself chief martial law administrator.

Zia focused his efforts on moving Pakistan closer to Islamic ideals. Islamic laws, called the sharia, were used to settle some legal disputes. Wardens ensured that Muslims prayed the required number of times each day. Women lost some of the rights they had gained under Ayub Khan.

Recent Events

In the early 1980s, a coalition of opposition groups formed the anti-Zia Movement for the Restoration of Democracy (MRD). One of the MRD's most visible members was Benazir Bhutto, the daughter of former prime minister Zulfikar Ali Bhutto. After returning to Pakistan from exile in

General Mohammed Zia ul-Haq came to power in 1979 as a result of a coup d'état. His rule was known for its strict control at the political and military levels. In August 1988, just before national elections, Zia and several highly placed military leaders were killed in an airplane crash.

1986, she became the leader of her father's party, the PPP.

In 1985, after assuming the presidency, Zia ended martial law. He allowed political parties to function openly and called for elections to the national assembly (the lower legislative house). The Muslim League won a majority of seats, and Zia chose Mohammed Khan Junejo as prime minister. In May 1988, however, Zia dissolved the cabinet, dismissed the prime minister, and suspended the national assembly. He cited widespread corruption as the reason for this move, although others believed it was Junejo's growing power that caused Zia to fire him. The president announced that new elections would be held in November.

In August 1988, President Zia and several top-ranking army officers died in an airplane crash. The disaster left Pakistan without strong leadership at the governmental and military levels.

Ghulam Ishaq Khan, chairman of the senate, took over as acting president. During the election campaign, the Muslim League split into two camps. Consequently, the PPP emerged at the forefront of political activity.

In November 1988, Ishaq Khan was elected president. The PPP won the largest number of seats of any of the nation's political organizations. The Muslim League and many small parties split the remainder. In accordance with the constitution, the president named Bhutto prime minister, and she became the first female head of an Islamic state.

As prime minister, Bhutto accomplished little for Pakistan. Hampered by opposing political forces, ethnic unrest, and her own political inexperience, Bhutto was for the most part unable to address the nation's problems. In August 1990, President Ishaq Khan, backed by the military, dissolved Benazir Bhutto's government, charging her administration with widespread corruption. In November 1990, Bhutto ran for office again and was defeated by

Photo by Reuters/Bettmann Newsphotos

Benazir Bhutto emerged as a likely candidate to replace Zia after his death in 1988.

Nawaz Sharif of the Islamic Democratic Alliance. Sharif implemented some badly needed economic reforms in Pakistan.

In May 1991, the National Assembly passed laws that made Pakistan's government consistent with Islamic law. Meanwhile, Sharif faced strong political tensions. Conflicts along party lines contributed to rivalries among officials. A split between President Khan and the prime minister came to a head in March 1993, when Sharif began talks about reducing the president's power over the government. President Khan dismissed Sharif and dissolved the National Assembly. But Pakistan's Supreme Court ruled that Khan's act was unconstitutional and ordered the old government to be restored. Khan complied, but his supporters dissolved Pakistan's provincial (state) governments. Sharif tried to gain control of the province of Punjab, but the people would not accept him as their governor.

Soon Pakistan's army intervened to negotiate an end to the crisis. The president and prime minister resigned, and the legislature was dissolved. An interim government took control of Pakistan until elections could be held.

In October 1991, Benazir Bhutto again was elected prime minister. The following month, Farooq Legari was elected president.

Along with lingering political difficulties, Bhutto faced growing violence among ethnic and religious groups, an economy in recession, and poor relations with the United States. During her term, Bhutto decreased Pakistan's budget deficit. She also smoothed U.S. ties strained by Pakistan's potential to create nuclear weapons. Despite these positive changes, Bhutto was dismissed again in late 1996, under charges of corruption and incompetence. President Legari appointed an interim prime minister and called for new elections.

Political turmoil and Islamic fundamentalism continues to destabilize the country. The challenge for Pakistan is to find the balance between Islam and democracy.

Government

Pakistan's Constitution of 1973 calls for a ceremonial president who is elected by the legislature. A controversial amendment, added in 1985, gives the president broad control over the government, including the power to officials and to dismiss the prime minister and the National Assembly.

The prime minister heads the government. Voters cast their ballots for the party of their choice, and the leader of the winning party becomes prime minister.

Pakistan's legislative system has two parts. The Senate has 87 members who serve six-year terms. The 217 members of the National Assembly have a maximum term of five years.

A supreme court and an Islamic court are the highest tribunals in Pakistan. A high court is at the top of the judicial system in each province.

A shop in Karachi sells wreaths and other finery for special occasions, such as the many public holidays and Muslim festivals (called eids).

3) The People

The population of Pakistan is 133.5 million, a figure that includes more than 1.4 million refugees from Afghanistan. Most Pakistanis live in rural areas and work as farmers or herders. Increasing numbers of people live in cities, where they usually work in factories or shops. Wealthy Pakistanis are often active in politics or education.

Ethnic Groups

Ethnically, Pakistan is very diverse, and each group retains its own dialect, culture, and history. Punjabis, the nation's largest ethnic community, live in Punjab—the biggest and most fertile province in the country. Even before Partition, Punjabis dominated the economy of their region. Punjabi landowners, whose estates produce much of the nation's food and exports, have become powerful members of the government. The continued influence of Punjabis over nearly every facet of national activity has created tensions between them and the other ethnic communities in Pakistan.

As a Punjabi, this man belongs to Pakistan's most influential ethnic group.

The Sindhi, residents of Sind, make up the country's second largest ethnic group. Less fertile than Punjab, Sind has fewer large plantations, and most of its residents farm small holdings. At independence, millions of Hindus and Sikhs left Sind for India, and a huge influx of refugee Muslims arrived from India. These newcomers possessed better schooling and more technical skills than the original Sindhi. Tensions now exist between the "new Sindhi" and the province's original inhabitants.

Pathans—who share cultural and linguistic ties with Pathans in Afghanistan—overwhelmingly populate the NWFP. Pathans have a variety of professions within the mountainous terrain of their province. The most important feature of

A Sindhi offers a parrot for sale on a Karachi street.

Wearing turbans, two Pathans intently discuss the price of an item in a Peshawar bazaar (market).

Pathan life is the Islamic religion. The Koran, or book of Islamic holy writings, influences many aspects of Pathan society, including the times for prayer and fasting and certain restrictions placed on men and women.

Pakistan's Baluchi population—most of whom are nomadic herders, farmers, or fishermen—is the largest in the world. The violent confrontation in the 1970s between some Baluchi and Pakistan's army angered even those Baluchi who had been content with life in Baluchistan. As a result, the Baluchi strongly oppose Pakistani and Punjabi attempts to control them.

Muhajirs—people who moved from India to Pakistan at Partition—generally migrated to urban areas and greatly increased the populations of Pakistan's cities. Many muhajirs have become powerful business and political leaders. Mohammed Ali Jinnah, Liaquat Ali Khan, and Mohammed Zia ul-Haq were all muhajirs.

Language and Literature

Shortly after Partition in 1947, the government of Pakistan sought to establish a national language. This proved to be difficult because Pakistanis speak many different tongues. The main language groups are Panjabi, Pashto (the Pathan tongue), Sindhi, and Baluchi. The dialects within these groups are also quite varied. The inhabitants of the city of Multan, for example, cannot easily understand the people of Lahore, even though both speak a form of Panjabi and live fewer than 200 miles apart.

Courtesy of Pakistan Tourism Development Corporation

These Baluchi children—who share ethnic backgrounds with peoples in Afghanistan and Iran—are dressed in the traditional clothing worn in the province of Baluchistan.

A man and his family rest beneath a sign written in Urdu—Pakistan's official language. The message encourages the use of family planning to curb the nation's high birthrate.

The government selected Urdu as Pakistan's official language because people who spoke different tongues could readily understand it. Yet Urdu is the main language of very few Pakistanis. A relatively new speech, Urdu is actually a blend of many languages that have Hindi as their primary grammatical base. Persian, Arabic, Turkish, and English words also contribute to the language.

Of all literary forms, poetry is the most popular among Pakistanis. People memorize long passages from the works of their most popular poets—Shah Abdul Latif, Khushal Khan Khattak, Muhammad Iqbal, and Faiz Ahmed Faiz. A favorite form of entertainment, especially among educated people, is the *mushaira,* at which a group of 20 or more people gathers to read poetry in sessions that can go on for several hours. Rural people enjoy telling folk stories, which include plays based on legendary or historical events.

Religion

According to a recent estimate, 97 percent of Pakistan's population are Muslim. The nation was created so that the Muslims of the subcontinent would have their own homeland. As a result, Islam holds a central place in Pakistani society, although ethnic affiliations also are important. Under the country's constitution, the president must be a Muslim, and all laws

Among popular Pakistani literary works are stories inspired by historical events. This painting—based on a poetic account—illustrates the romance between Prince Salim (who became Emperor Jahangir) and a young woman.

Tirich Mir—the highest peak in the Hindu Kush—rises behind the Juma Masjid (a mosque), which stands on the banks of the Mastuj River in Chitral.

must be in accordance with the principles of Islam.

Soon after the prophet Muhammad founded Islam in Saudi Arabia in the seventh century, the religion split into two main factions—Sunnis and Shiites. Sunni Muslims accept an elected successor to the Islamic leadership, while Shiites regard only descendants of Muhammad as legitimate. Most of Pakistan's Muslims belong to the Sunni sect. Shiites are concentrated in Karachi and make up substantial parts of the religious communities in Punjab and the NWFP.

Muslims of both sects are required to pray five times daily and to observe rules of fasting, especially during the holy month of Ramadan. They must make charitable donations and are encouraged to attempt a pilgrimage to the holy city of Mecca in Saudi Arabia once in their lifetime. In recent times, conservative Pakistani Muslims have been in conflict with religious moderates over the role of Islam

In preparation for entering a mosque, this Muslim washes his face, hands, and feet at a public water fountain.

in an Islamic republic. The conservatives want all laws in the country to conform to Islamic principles. Moderates accept a mixture of civil and religious regulations.

Small numbers of Hindus and Christians live in Pakistan. Laws bar them from holding public office, although they are generally free to practice their faiths. Some discrimination in employment and educational opportunities exists against non-Muslims.

The Arts

Pakistanis excel in the arts of painting, weaving, music, and dance. Working on handlooms, villagers weave fine cottons and then paint or stamp bright designs on the cloth. Craftspeople also make charpoys—flat beds made of wood and either jute or leather. The wood forms the frame and the strips of jute or leather are interlaced to make the sleeping surface. Embroidery, leatherwork, miniature painting,

In the corner of a mosque (right), a man reads his Koran—the book of sacred writings that forms the basis of the Islamic religion. The Koran forbids representations of human figures in art. A building in Uch (below) displays the geometric patterns that have long been used in Islamic decoration.

Courtesy of Nathan Rabe

and ceramics continue to be popular art forms.

Because Islam forbids the use of human images to decorate mosques, geometric patterns commonly ornament the doorways, floors, and walls of these buildings. In addition, the many groups who once controlled lands in Pakistan have left beautiful architectural treasures that continue to influence modern designers.

Pakistan's ethnic groups enjoy both classical music and folk tunes. Drums and horns are popular folk instruments, and they provide accompaniment for graceful dances, such as the *luddi* and the *khattak*.

Health

Living conditions in Pakistan have improved since independence, but the nation

While watching a polo match—a sport requiring great skill on horseback—a Pakistani in Gilgit plays his horn.

The seventeenth-century Shalamar Gardens in Lahore is one of Pakistan's architectural treasures. Its style has influenced modern designers and builders.

A line of patients waits outside a doctor's office. Despite improvements in medical care since independence, Pakistanis continue to suffer from malnutrition, diphtheria, and malaria.

In Lahore, a woman uses a public well to do her family's laundry. Unsafe water – for both drinking and cooking purposes – is a major cause of disease in Pakistan.

still must deal with the problems caused by an inadequate level of health care. The situation for women is generally worse than it is for men. For example, female children less frequently receive medical treatment and often are given smaller amounts of food than their brothers.

The major health dangers—disease, malnutrition, and impure water—are the same ones that existed in the 1950s. Diseases like malaria, typhoid, and tuberculosis still afflict the population. Even curable ailments, such as diphtheria and measles, continue to kill Pakistani children.

The infant mortality rate—91 deaths in every 1,000 live births—is higher than the average for southern Asia. About two-thirds of the population do not have access to safe drinking water. Life expectancy in Pakistan is 61 years—an average figure in southern Asia. Almost half of the population are under the age of 15, and only 3 percent are over age 65.

49

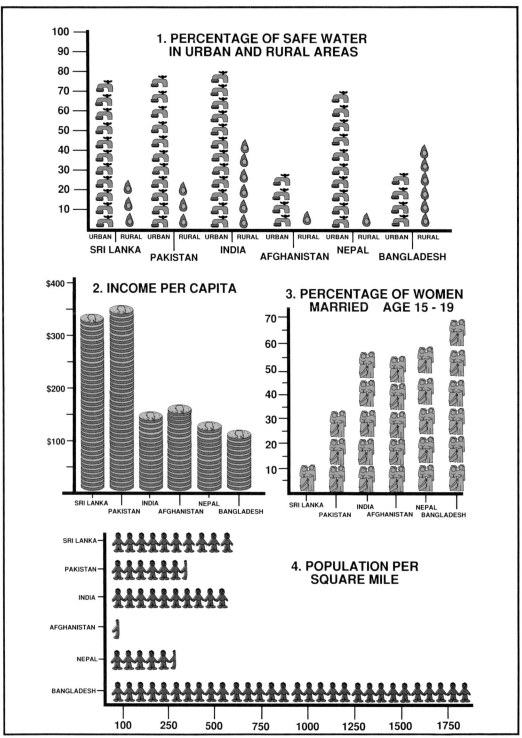

1. PERCENTAGE OF SAFE WATER IN URBAN AND RURAL AREAS

	URBAN	RURAL
SRI LANKA		
PAKISTAN		
INDIA		
AFGHANISTAN		
NEPAL		
BANGLADESH		

2. INCOME PER CAPITA

SRI LANKA, PAKISTAN, INDIA, AFGHANISTAN, NEPAL, BANGLADESH

3. PERCENTAGE OF WOMEN MARRIED   AGE 15 - 19

SRI LANKA, PAKISTAN, INDIA, AFGHANISTAN, NEPAL, BANGLADESH

4. POPULATION PER SQUARE MILE

SRI LANKA, PAKISTAN, INDIA, AFGHANISTAN, NEPAL, BANGLADESH

100   250   500   750   1000   1250   1500   1750

Artwork by Mindy A. Rabin

Depicted in this chart are factors relating to the standard of living in six countries in southern Asia. Information taken from "1987 World Population Data Sheet," "The World's Women: A Profile," and "Children of the World" compiled by the Population Reference Bureau, Washington, D.C.

Islamia College in Peshawar is among Pakistan's institutions of higher learning.

Education

Although the government guarantees every child in Pakistan a free primary education, school attendance is not required, and universal schooling has not yet been achieved. Moreover, Islamic tradition, which urges females to remain in the home, makes it difficult for girls to obtain a basic education.

In the middle 1990s, about 16 million children attended primary and midlevel schools. With Pakistan's population growing at 3 percent—one of the highest annual rates in southern Asia—the number of school-age children is large, yet fewer than half actually attend classes.

The government has begun a public campaign to increase literacy, which in the middle 1990s was about 47 percent for men and about 21 percent for women. One recent development is the nationally funded *Nai Roshani* (New Light) schools that dot the countryside. They provide free education to adults and children.

Pakistan began with few institutions of higher learning and now has many universities, colleges, and technical-training schools. The University of Punjab in

Pakistani children study in an open-air classroom. About twice as many boys as girls attend school.

Lahore and the University of Karachi are among the nation's main postsecondary institutions. Yet to enter into any program that ensures well-paid employment after graduation—engineering or computer science, for example—students must pay bribes to officials. The result is that a university education is available mainly to the children of wealthy people.

Food and Clothing

Pakistani cuisine, although basically spicy, is also known for its richness. The more popular dishes are pilau (specially cooked meat and rice), *kofta* (meatballs), and *murgh-i-mussalam* (stuffed fried chicken). Sweets typically include *zarda*, made with sweet rice, nuts, and spices; *korma*, a mixture of tiny spaghetti noodles, sugar, and nuts; and halvah, composed of ground carrots, sugar, nuts, and spices.

Chapati—flat rounds of bread usually made of whole wheat—form the basis of almost every meal in Pakistan. In poor households, chapati are often the main course. They are served with other foods spread thinly over the bread like butter.

For both men and women, the most frequently worn style of Pakistani dress is the *shalwar-qamiz*, a combination of loose trousers and a long blouse. Women sometimes add a scarf, which they wrap around their shoulders and head. Some women have also adopted a veil or even a full-length covering called a burka in accordance with Islamic rules of modesty. Men often wear turbans or caps.

Photo by Bernice K. Condit

Photo by Bill Kish

After pulling off bits of dough from a larger piece and flattening them, this Pakistani cook is ready to make chapati—fried rounds of wheat bread that are eaten with most meals.

Some burkas cover the head, body, and face. Vision is possible through a mesh that is fitted over the area of the eyes.

52

A worker sorts pine seedlings at a nursery run by the Kohistan Development Board. Since independence in 1947, Pakistan's government has initiated projects to improve economic conditions throughout the nation. The program in Kohistan, NWFP, focuses on conservation and reforestation, among other goals.

4) The Economy

At the time of Partition in 1947, Pakistan's economy was almost exclusively agricultural. There were no large industries, no locally owned banks, few commercial enterprises, and only a handful of trained technicians, professional people, and skilled workers. Since Partition, new banks, businesses, and industries have sprung up, and part of the work force has undergone technical training.

The number of jobs requiring skilled workers has risen in Pakistan, and many unskilled Pakistanis have left to take better-paying jobs in other Islamic countries. Over two million Pakistanis work abroad, mostly in oil-producing countries throughout the Middle East. The economy of Pakistan benefits substantially from the foreign earnings that these laborers send home to their families.

Since 1955 Pakistan's economic development has followed a series of five-year plans. These long-range strategies name specific economic goals, identify resources, and assign priorities. To achieve its economic aims, Pakistan has sometimes relied heavily on economic assistance from more developed countries—including the United States, Great Britain, Australia, New Zealand, and Canada.

53

Agriculture

Despite advances in some industrial and technical fields, Pakistan is still a predominantly agricultural country. Most Pakistanis make their living from the land, and agriculture provides 30 percent of the nation's yearly income. Cultivation methods are still generally traditional, however, and poor irrigation techniques affect annual yields. Substantial amounts of productive land have been lost because the government has not maintained the British-built canal system that once irrigated Punjab and Sind—some of Asia's most productive agricultural land.

FOOD CROPS

Pakistan's principal food crops are wheat and rice. Farmers also grow other cereals, such as millet, sorghum, corn, and barley. In addition to grains, chick-peas (called gram in Pakistan) have become an important crop.

Wheat fields grew from 11.3 million acres in 1961 to 17.7 million acres in 1983, but Pakistan still imported wheat during those years. High-quality seeds and better fertilizers increased annual yields of the crop, and, between 1961 and 1990, wheat yields rose from 3.8 million tons to 15 million tons. By the early 1990s, the nation

Courtesy of Clarice Wilson

Terraced wheat and rice fields, which are irrigated by melting snows, stretch across a valley near Chitral.

A streetside market displays the variety of fruits and vegetables available from Pakistan's farms.

had become self-sufficient in its wheat production and had begun to export small amounts of the grain.

Rice, another important food crop in Pakistan, covered about five million acres in the early 1990s. Farmers grow rice on terraces and in irrigated fields, and tonnages have increased with the use of better-quality rice strains. Pakistan exports about a million tons of rice each year, making the nation a major supplier of this grain on the world market.

Dwarfed by the surrounding plants, a woman near the Afghan border tends her field.

High-yielding rice strains have increased Pakistan's crop volumes in recent years.

Near Thal, in northwestern Pakistan, workers load sugarcane stalks onto a tractor-drawn cart. Despite drops in world sugar prices, sugarcane is still a major export crop.

EXPORT CROPS

Cash crops, grown on large estates for export, include cotton, sugarcane, rice, tobacco, and oilseeds. In the early 1990s, more than seven million acres were devoted to export crops, with cotton being among the most valuable products. Workers handpick about 1.5 million tons of cotton each year.

After independence, the number of acres planted in sugarcane increased until Pakistan began to produce too much sugar for the international market. Farmers responded by decreasing their sugarcane fields, although a record 37 million tons of cane was harvested in 1989, despite low sugar prices on the world market.

Tobacco and oilseeds make up the remainder of Pakistan's major cash crops. The number of acres devoted to these crops is relatively small.

LIVESTOCK

Livestock raising has long been the livelihood of Pakistanis in Baluchistan and the NWFP, where crop cultivation is impossible because of the dry climate and the rugged terrain. Herders tend flocks of sheep and goats and may raise cattle as work animals. Grazing land is limited, and farmers have not introduced improved animal breeds into their herds. As a result, livestock raising is still a small-scale enterprise in Pakistan.

At Multan, gatherers sort and stack wool, which has been sheared from locally raised sheep.

Goats scramble over a narrow bridge in the NWFP, where herding is one of the main professions.

HASHISH AND OPIATE PRODUCTION AND SUPPLY, 1986

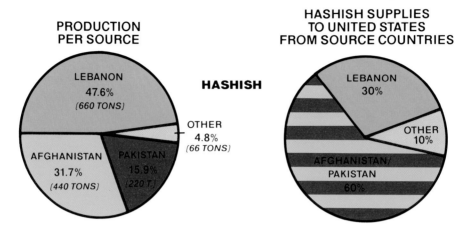

PRODUCTION PER SOURCE

HASHISH SUPPLIES TO UNITED STATES FROM SOURCE COUNTRIES

HASHISH

LEBANON
47.6%
(660 TONS)

OTHER
4.8%
(66 TONS)

AFGHANISTAN
31.7%
(440 TONS)

PAKISTAN
15.9%
(220 T.)

LEBANON
30%

OTHER
10%

AFGHANISTAN/
PAKISTAN
60%

(India and Nepal consume and export domestically grown hashish, but to what extent is unknown. Over six tons of hashish originating in India were seized in North America in 1986.)

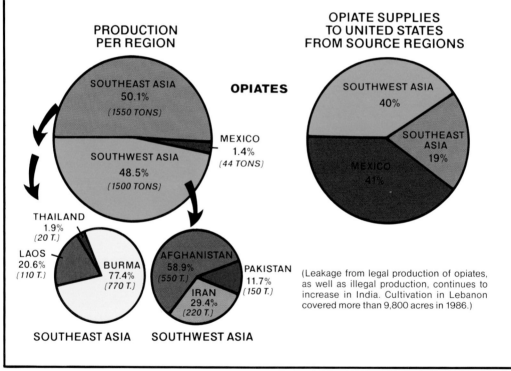

PRODUCTION PER REGION

OPIATE SUPPLIES TO UNITED STATES FROM SOURCE REGIONS

OPIATES

SOUTHEAST ASIA
50.1%
(1550 TONS)

MEXICO
1.4%
(44 TONS)

SOUTHWEST ASIA
48.5%
(1500 TONS)

SOUTHWEST ASIA
40%

SOUTHEAST
ASIA
19%

MEXICO
41%

THAILAND
1.9%
(20 T.)

LAOS
20.6%
(110 T.)

BURMA
77.4%
(770 T.)

AFGHANISTAN
58.9%
(550 T.)

PAKISTAN
11.7%
(150 T.)

IRAN
29.4%
(220 T.)

SOUTHEAST ASIA   SOUTHWEST ASIA

(Leakage from legal production of opiates, as well as illegal production, continues to increase in India. Cultivation in Lebanon covered more than 9,800 acres in 1986.)

Artwork by Elizabeth Pilon

These pie charts depict data about both the production and U.S. supplies of two kinds of drugs. Hashish is a substance taken from the *Cannabis sativa* plant, which also is a source of marijuana. Opiates are drugs that come from opium poppies *(Papaver somniferum)*, mostly in the refined forms of opium and heroin. The production pies *(left)* cover the percentages estimated to be manufactured by each country or region. The pies depicting U.S. supplies *(right)* illustrate only percentages that arrive in the United States. They do not include amounts used within source countries or regions, nor do they illustrate percentages that go to other parts of the world. Data taken from the *NNICC Report, 1985-1986* compiled by the U.S. Drug Enforcement Administration, Washington, D.C.

The government has tried to stop harvests of opium poppies—the plants from which the drugs opium and heroin are made. The administration's efforts have reduced illegal crops in some areas. Yet in 1985 estimates indicated that Pakistan earned $10 billion from its export of heroin—a figure that is twice what the nation generated from its legitimate exports.

Laboratories that refine poppies—which come from both Afghanistan and Pakistan—into heroin are generally located in the NWFP near the Afghan border. Although some heroin stays in Pakistan, much of the drug crosses the border to India or is smuggled to countries in Europe, North America, and the Persian Gulf.

Mining and Industry

Although rich in minerals, Pakistan has not taken advantage of its natural resources. The nation lacks machinery, roads, and funds to develop this sector of its economy.

Photo by Bill Kish

Opium poppies grow best with little water and care. As a result, they are widely cultivated in areas where other crops cannot survive without irrigation and constant attention.

Large deposits of chromite (from which chrome is made), copper, bauxite (the raw material for aluminum), graphite, and natural gas are located in Baluchistan. The Baluchi, however, are reluctant to allow the government to extract the minerals in Baluchistan. They fear that the revenue from the deposits would enrich only wealthy Punjabis.

Despite these difficulties the government built the Saindak mining project in Baluchistan to extract copper, iron ore, sulfur, gold, silver, and molybdenum (used to strengthen steel) from the region. Foreign firms have been encouraged to provide machinery and expertise in exchange for mining rights. The government also

Courtesy of OPIC

As evidence of Pakistan's growing industrial base, workers at a chemical company assemble packages of medicine.

59

At a plant in Lahore, a worker sends cardboard through a press that imprints trademark names and symbols on boxes before they are put together.

built the Sui gas line, which transports natural gas from deposits in Baluchistan to major urban centers.

After independence, Pakistan vowed to industrialize rapidly. By the early 1990s, industry supplied 18 percent of the gross domestic product (the value of goods and services produced by a country in a year). Compared to other developing countries, manufacturing in Pakistan is growing quickly. Textiles head the list of manufactured products and include both factory-made and hand-woven fabrics. Other items include processed foods and cement.

Using its natural gas and limestone, Pakistan produces ammonia-based fertilizers. Pakistan also manufactures large quantities of penicillin and other medical compounds from its crop of artemisia (a strong-smelling herb).

The textile industry thrives in Karachi, where a weaver oversees the production of another bolt of cloth.

Karachi's port has been upgraded in recent years to include shipbuilding and maintenance facilities.

In both the private and public sectors of the economy, the government's principal goal is to reduce the country's dependence on foreign imports, mostly of raw materials for manufactured goods. A notably successful project is a shipyard in Karachi, which first went into production in 1956. This well-equipped installation builds vessels and does ship repairs of all kinds. With the help of the Soviet Union, Pakistan built a major steel plant in Karachi in the early 1980s. Other industrial complexes produce machine tools, electrical equipment, and heavy castings.

Energy and Transportation

In the late 1940s, forests were Pakistan's main fuel base. In the 1990s, modern sources—hydroelectric power and natural

Wood still fulfills some of Pakistan's energy needs. Lumber—taken from dwindling forests—is also used as construction material.

61

Located near Islamabad, the huge Tarbela Dam uses the waters of the Indus River to power hydroelectric plants that serve the needs of central Pakistan.

gas, for example—provided the nation with household energy. Residents in rural areas continue to use wood and dung as fuel, and much of Pakistan's landscape has been stripped of trees. Commercial energy, which powers industry and transportation, comes mainly from natural gas, oil, hydroelectricity, and coal. The Tarbela Dam on the Indus River and the Mangla Dam on the Jhelum River have doubled Pakistan's hydropower output.

Lack of a well-organized transportation network hampers Pakistan's economic development. The country has about

In dry areas of the nation, camels *(right)* are a common means of transportation. In the mountains, snow and rocks *(below)* often impede road travel.

63,000 miles of roads, 40 percent of which are paved. Few people own cars, and most rural travel is accomplished on camels, on donkeys, or on foot. About 5,500 miles of railroad track crisscross Pakistan, connecting major cities to one another.

Pakistan International Airlines handles the nation's overseas flights, and airports that can accommodate jets are located in Karachi, Lahore, and Rawalpindi. Karachi serves as the nation's main seaport. Smaller ports also exist, notably at Port Muhammad bin Qasim, which opened in the 1980s.

The Future

The collapse of the Soviet Union in 1991 led to the end of Pakistan's military involvement in Afghanistan. However, many Afghan Islamic fundamentalists who ran their military operations from Pakistan have remained within the country's borders. Their attention has turned from the Afghan conflicts to acts of terrorism against perceived threats to Islamic order.

The United States suspended financial aid to Pakistan during the early 1990s, when Pakistan would not confirm that it was not building nuclear weapons. By 1993, relations between the two countries were strained. When Benazir Bhutto took office, she reestablished friendly ties by verifying that Pakistan had nuclear capabilities and by agreeing to work with the United States on reducing or eliminating the need to develop Pakistan's nuclear program. As a result, the United States resumed some of the financial aid.

While addressing the nation's economic problems, Pakistanis must fully decide what influence Islam will have on their government. They must also find a way to balance the demands of the country's various ethnic communities. Avoiding a war with India over the disputed territory of Jammu and Kashmir grows more difficult as the Jammu and Kashmir Liberation Front, backed by Muslim Kashmiris, becomes more aggressive. Until Pakistan resolves these long-standing issues, the nation's future will remain uncertain.

Photo by Wide World Photos

Benazir Bhutto (center with raised hand) **drew large crowds during the national campaign in 1988. She has twice served as Pakistan's prime minister and is the first woman in the world to head an Islamic country.**

Index

24862